GREAT SCIENTISTS
MARIE CURIE

STEVE PARKER

Belitha Press

This edition published in 2003 by
Belitha Press
A member of **Chrysalis** Books plc
64 Brewery Road, London N7 9NT

Typeset by Chambers Wallace, London
Printed in Malaysia

British Library Cataloguing in Publication Data
for this book is available from the British Library.

ISBN 1 84138 623 5

Acknowledgements

Photographic credits:
AIP Niels Bohr Library 11 bottom right Lande
    Collection, 19 bottom UK Atomic Energy
    Authority
Barnaby's Picture Library 22
Bridgeman Art Library 8 bottom
Mary Evans Picture Library 11 top, 15 bottom left
L'Illustration/Sygma 16 bottom left, 24 top,
    26 bottom
Musee Curie, Paris title page, 8 top, 9 right, 17 top,
    26 top
Popperfoto/Marie Curie Collection 2, 5, 9 left,
    6, 10, 12, 13, 16 top and middle right, 19 top, 20,
    23, 24 bottom, 25
Science Photo Library 4 Martin Bond, 11 bottom
    left J-L Charmet, 15 top Martin Bond and
    bottom right Alexander Tsiaras, 17 bottom
    J-L Charmet, 27 top Los Alamos National
    Laboratory and bottom J-L Charmet

Cover montage images supplied by Mary Evans
Picture Library and Ann Ronan Picture Library

Illustrations: Tony Smith 6-7, 14, 22-23
Rodney Shackell 13, 18, 21, 25
Editor: Kate Scarborough
Designer: Andrew Oliver
Picture researcher: Vanessa Kelly

*The statue of Marie Curie
to be found in Warsaw, the
city of her childhood.*

Contents

Introduction

The 20th century has been called The Atomic Age. As it began, scientists were trying to find out if **atoms**, which they had thought were the smallest particles of a substance, were made up of even smaller particles. They succeeded in splitting the atom in 1919. This knowledge has produced the terrifying weapon of the atomic bomb. It has also led to atomic or **nuclear** power, with its benefits and drawbacks.

Marie Curie was one of the first people to research radioactivity. She discovered the substance radium, which naturally gives off radioactivity as its atoms split apart. She carried out her research at a time when the nature of radioactivity was not really understood. She also had to struggle against lack of money and recognition, against illness, and against those who mistakenly believed that a woman could not be a real scientist.

Eventually Marie Curie became world-famous and won two **Nobel** Prizes. She raised much money for research and founded scientific organizations. From her work, and that of her colleagues, today we have a much greater understanding of atoms and radioactivity.

Marie Curie's research helped scientists towards splitting the atom, to produce nuclear energy. Today, nuclear power stations like the one below generate huge quantities of electricity.

Chapter One
The Early Years

Maria Sklodowska was born at this site, 16 Freta Street, Warsaw. The building has been converted to a museum in memory of her life and work.

The Sklodowska children. Marie was the youngest of the family. Oldest sister Sofia is on the left, with brother Jozef sitting on the table.

On 7 November 1867, a baby girl was born in Freta Street, Warsaw, Poland. She was named Maria Salomee Sklodowska, though her family would call her Manya (her name is sometimes written Marya Sklodovska). Her parents were teachers in Warsaw. They already had four children, daughters Sofia, Bronislawa (Bronia) and Helena, and son Jozef.

At the time, Poland was under the rule of neighbouring Russia. The best education and the best jobs went to Russians. Most Polish people were poor and life was tough. However with two teachers as parents, Maria and her family were better off than many others.

Family life in Warsaw

Maria (on the left), her father, and her two surviving sisters. (Sofia died in 1876.) This photograph was taken just before Bronia on the right of her father left to study in Paris.

The children had a good education. They were brought up strictly and encouraged to work hard, to respect their elders, and to be religious. They had caring parents, but they noticed that their mother suddenly stopped kissing or even hugging them. She had caught the then incurable disease of **tuberculosis**, and did not want to pass the germs to her children. In 1876 Marie's oldest sister Sofia died of typhus. Two years later her mother died.

In 1883 Maria finished her school education. She had shown herself to be a hard worker, clever, able to concentrate hard and with a very good memory. She won a gold medal at her school, the Russian Lycée. But she became ill with what she called "the fatigue of growth and study", and spent a year recovering with relatives in the country.

On her return to Warsaw, Maria and her sister Bronia began to attend secret meetings of the **"Floating University"**. The members read about scientific and other work which was banned by the Russians because they considered it might stir up rebellious ideas. In 1885, to help with family finances, Maria became a **governess**.

When Maria travelled from Warsaw to Paris, she took everything she would need – including a stove, and even parts of her bed.

From pupil to teacher

She worked for several families, teaching and looking after the children. In her spare time she taught herself maths and physics. She sent some of her wages to her sister Bronia, who had gone to Paris to study medicine. (Later, Bronia would help Maria with money for her studies.)

In 1890 her father obtained a better job, and the family's money worries lessened. Maria lived with him for a while and also taught the sciences. She began to consider going to university in Paris, like her sister, since Warsaw University did not admit women. And so in 1891, Maria Sklodowska went to Paris by third-class train, to study for maths and physics degrees.

Great Thinkers of the Time

Maria read the works of many scientists and other famous thinkers, even though the Russians tried to ban them in Poland.

● The English naturalist Charles Darwin had written about **evolution** and the struggle for survival, in his book *On The Origin of Species* (1859). His work led many scientists to doubt the existence of a God, and this greatly affected Maria.

● The French thinker Auguste Comte wrote about *Positive Philosophy* in the 1830-40s. Maria and her friends in the Floating University called themselves "**positivists**" and followed his ideas, since they fitted in with their hopes of getting rid of the Russians and leaving Poland free once again.

● Maria also studied how scientists should think clearly and logically, carry out experiments, and test their ideas and theories. By her middle teens she was no longer religious. Her scientific mind could not believe in something that could not be proved. Eventually science was to take over from religion and politics in Maria's life.

Maria worked hard while at University. Her French was not good, and she had only a small circle of friends. She rarely enjoyed the stylish Paris lifestyle shown in the painting below, by Edmond Georges Grandjean.

Chapter Two
Paris

At first Maria stayed with her sister Bronia and her doctor husband in Paris. But she soon moved to the student area, living in a tiny attic with no proper lighting and only a coal stove. She had very little money, ate poorly, had to pay for her lessons, and worked long hours in the library. Yet she found her work so satisfying that the hardships were worthwhile.

Maria studied at the Sorbonne (Paris University) under some of the most famous mathematicians and physicists of the time, including Paul Appel and Gabriel Lippmann. In 1893 she gained her physics degree. She obtained the highest marks in her group, and began to work in Lippmann's **laboratory**. The next year she gained her maths degree, coming second in her group. Now she planned to do pure scientific research, for the love of her subject and the joy of increased knowledge, rather than for any money that could be made from it.

Pierre Curie

Pierre Curie was born in 1859 in Paris, and educated by his father, a physician. Even as a schoolboy of 14 he was deeply interested in mathematics. In 1878 he became a laboratory assistant at the Paris University. With his brother Jacques he studied heat, crystals, magnetism and electricity. Four years later he became supervisor at the École de Physique (School of Physics).

The Curies prepare for a cycle ride, from the garden of their house at Boulevard Kellerman. Cycling was one of their many shared loves.

Research and marriage

At the age of 27, Maria met Pierre Curie at the home of a Polish physicist. He was 35, a senior worker in a physics laboratory. They had much in common, including a love of nature and the countryside, little need for wealth and the comforts of life, and a great passion for physics research.

Pierre wrote letters of love and physics experiments to Maria. The next year, on 26 July 1895, they were married in Sceaux, Pierre's home town near Paris. Maria Sklodowska became Marie Curie. Their honeymoon was the first of many bicycle trips around France together, enjoying the fresh air and countryside, and recovering from the long hours in laboratories and libraries.

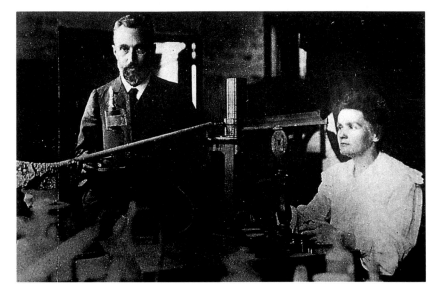

Pierre and Marie photographed in their laboratory, in 1898. This was about the time she was purifying uranium ore to find the mystery radioactive substance.

On 12 September 1897 Irène Curie was born. A few months after she was born, Marie published her first scientific work – her report on the magnetic properties of steel.

The Curies at work

Both Marie and Pierre loved their research for the way it advanced scientific knowledge. Pierre had worked his way up by jobs helping in laboratories, not as a student. He published his important findings regularly in scientific journals, but he did not try to sell them to make money from them, and he refused payments and loans for research. Despite his scientific successes, the university superiors did not choose him for a more important post because, in their view, he did not have the proper qualifications such as a science degree.

In 1895, however, Pierre Curie gained a doctor of science award for his earlier work on magnetism. Marie went to work with him at the Ecole after their marriage. She studied the magnetic **properties** of various **alloys** (combinations of metals), and wrote the first of her dozens of scientific publications.

Rays and radiation

Meanwhile, in November 1895 Wilhelm Röntgen, a German physicist, discovered invisible "**penetrating rays**" coming from an electric tube in one of his experiments. He called them X-rays, because he did not know what they were. They could pass through flesh and other substances, but not through hard, dense materials like bone and thick metals.

X-rays and their effects became world-famous within months. Marie and Pierre Curie followed the new discoveries about "strange **emissions**" with interest, as they studied and prepared lectures at their plainly-furnished apartment in the Rue de la Glaciere.

In 1896 the French physicist Henri Becquerel discovered more kinds of penetrating rays. Unlike Röntgen's, which were made by an electrical effect, these rays seemed to come naturally from a piece of **uranium**. Becquerel had left the uranium lying on a sealed packet of photographic paper for several days in a drawer, and it caused the paper to mist over. Marie, looking for a new subject to study for her doctor of science award, chose the mysterious rays detected by Becquerel.

X-rays caused much interest and even amusement, as their "see-through" qualities became known to the public. This cartoon was published in 1900, five years after their discovery.

A New Kind of Ray

Wilhelm Röntgen (above) discovered X-rays while working as Professor of Physics at the University of Würzburg, Germany. He told hardly anyone about his findings for two months, as he worked day and night, trying to make sense of the discovery. One of the first X-ray images (below) was of his wife's hand and ring. Röntgen was awarded the first-ever Nobel Prize for Physics, in 1901.

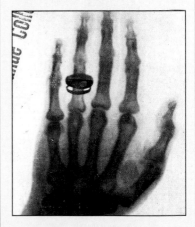

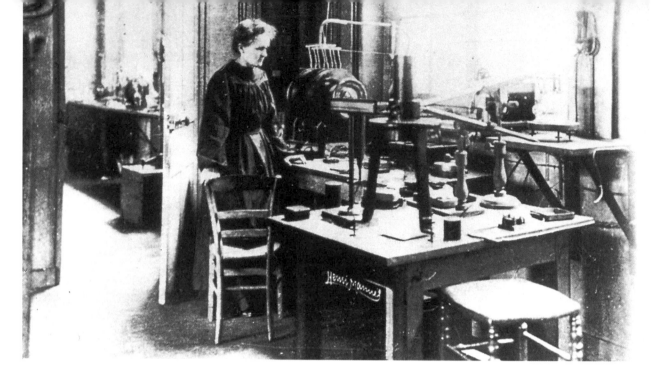

Marie worked hard in her "shed" behind the main physics buildings at the Paris University.

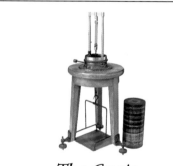

The Curie electrometer

Pierre and Jacques Curie invented their electrometer to find out whether a substance was giving off emissions or not. When a substance gives off radioactive emissions, the air around it carries electricity. This electricity is measured by the electrometer.

Chapter Three
The Discovery of Radium

For her laboratory, Marie was offered a small, damp, unheated room in the École de Physique. She had no money for her research, and she worked with equipment and materials given by colleagues.

Using the **electrometer** invented by Pierre and his brother Jacques, she began to look for other substances that gave off emissions, like uranium did. She discovered that a substance called thorium was one of them. She also found that it did not matter how uranium and substances containing it were treated, they always gave off the same amount of emissions.

Marie reasoned that the emissions could not be caused by chemical reactions, otherwise they would change as the uranium was added to or separated from other chemicals. Could they be coming from the smallest particles of uranium itself – its atoms? This idea went against all the scientific theories of the time, but it proved to be true. Marie and Pierre also became interested in the luminous effects of the newly discovered emissions, since they caused certain substances to glow.

Too many emissions

Marie's main source of uranium was pitchblende, an ore (the natural, unpurified mixture of rocks and other substances, as mined from the Earth). The mineral **chalcolite** also contained uranium. In 1898, her tests and calculations showed that pitchblende and chalcolite gave off more emissions than expected from the amount of uranium they contained. There must be another substance in the ore mixture, which gave off the extra emissions.

Finding the mystery substance

Marie began the chemical procedures to find the mystery substance. It was hard physical work. She ground the ore, sieved it, dissolved it by boiling, boiled off the liquid, filtered it, **distilled** it, and passed electricity through it. She and her colleagues checked the contents and purity at each stage.

After each stage, Marie took the part that gave off most emissions, and purified it further. Finally she made a pure version of the new substance, which was a metal – a new chemical **element**. In great excitement she called it polonium, after her homeland of Poland. In the scientific report of her work, she invented the word *radio-active*, describing substances like uranium and polonium that gave off the penetrating rays or radiation.

*A page from one of Marie's laboratory notebooks, containing mathematical **equations** about energy emissions.*

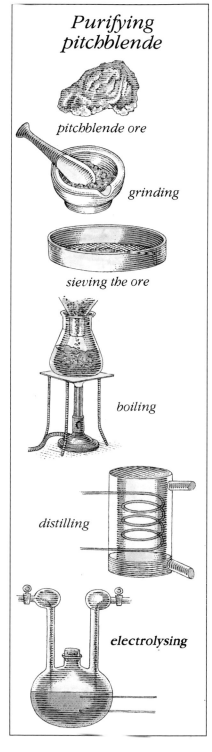

Purifying pitchblende

pitchblende ore

grinding

sieving the ore

boiling

distilling

electrolysing

Glowing in the dark

Polonium was the first highly radioactive element to be made in pure form. It gave off so much radiation that it made the surrounding air glow, and the polonium itself became hot.

But Marie's work had shown that polonium, though powerful, was not responsible for the rest of pitchblende's radioactivity. She continued her work and partly purified a substance which she thought contained another new element. This she named radium, after the Latin word *radius*, meaning "ray". However, there was so little of it in pitchblende, that huge amounts of ore would be needed to prepare a tiny pure sample of radium.

Some of the radioactive substances purified by the Curies gave off an eerie glow. Pierre kept a small glass container of the substance in his pocket, and brought it out at gatherings as a "party trick". His guests were amazed at the unearthly light.

The Race for radium

From 1899, Marie began the immense task of obtaining pure radium in some form, so proving its existence. Pierre was still lecturing and working at his own research, but he gradually became more and more interested in radioactivity. His chief task was to analyse the samples which Marie made at each stage of the process.

Tonnes of radioactive mine wastes arrived at the Paris laboratory, from Bohemia (now part of Czechoslovakia) and the Belgian Congo in Africa. Marie performed the chemical separation processes on bucketfuls of it. The final stages were difficult and kept going wrong. At the time, the hazards of working with radioactive materials were not fully known. For most of her adult life, Marie suffered ill health. She had the symptoms of tuberculosis after daughter Irène's birth, and soon she was feeling sick, tired and aching because of radiation poisoning. Her hands became stiff, cracked and ulcer-covered, as she mixed and boiled the radioactive materials. Even many years later, her notebooks and laboratory seat were highly radioactive.

It is remarkable that Marie was able to carry out such hard physical work, even with her long cycling breaks in the countryside. It is also remarkable that she lived so long. Many of her work colleagues died much younger.

Danger! Radioactive!

Today we are aware of the hazards of radioactivity (the above is the international warning symbol). In Marie Curie's time, the hazards were only just being revealed. Both the Curies refused to believe the dangers of radioactivity. Marie only accepted the dangers of radiation towards the end of her life. Today people wear protective clothing (see below) when working with radioactive materials.

The Curie family in a rare moment of relaxation. Both Marie and Pierre often looked tired and ill, from long periods of work and exposure to radioactivity.

Chapter Four

First Woman of Science

In later life, Marie Curie described the hard years of purifying radium as the best of her life. She looked after her family and home, but her research took up most of her time. Among her helpers were André Debierne (one of Pierre's students) and Gustave Bémont. She was a thorough worker and demanded high standards of cleanliness from her assistants in the laboratory – the "shed" behind the École de Physique.

While she was studying radium, Marie carried out other research. In 1899, with Henri Becquerel and another scientist, Fritz Giesel, she investigated the properties of the emissions themselves. Pierre became more interested in this part of the research.

Marie worked enormously hard in her laboratory and workshop at the Rue Lhomond, shown on the right. She was often tired, felt sick, and had painful joints and muscles. She suffered sore hands from radiation burns caused by the substances she worked with. At first she and Pierre thought these problems were due to the very long hours they spent on their research.

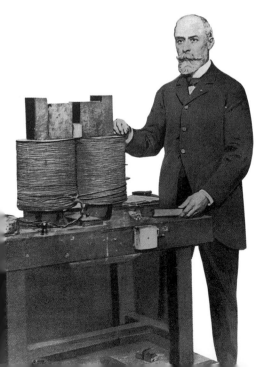

◄ *The French physicist Henri Becquerel, here standing next to a huge* **electromagnet,** *worked closely with the Curies. In 1896 he discovered the radioactive emissions of uranium, and together they showed that the beta rays or beta particles (see page 21) given off by radium were really streams of electrons, moving at high speed. Becquerel's work also led to the invention of the fluorescent light, and a unit in radiation physics is named after him.*

One-tenth of a gram

The next year, the Curies moved to Boulevard Kellerman in Paris. Eugene, Pierre's father, joined them to care for Irène. Pierre left his crystal research and began to study the properties of the radioactive emissions.

To help with the family income and provide money for research, Marie and Pierre both took extra jobs. She became a physics lecturer at an academy for girls in Sèvres. He took the additional post of Assistant Professor at the Polytechnique. Despite the Curies' increasing reputations in the scientific world, and their many achievements, the Paris University was very slow to recognize their work, and still provided no money for their research.

During the early 1900s, the Curies sent samples of their purified radioactive substances to laboratories in other countries. As a result, research on radioactivity leaped forwards and many other scientists became involved.

Eventually in 1902, Marie made a pure form of radium salt. There was only 0.1 gram – a small speck. (Seven tons of pitchblende yield 1 gram of radium.) Yet it was enough radium to work out some of its physical and chemical properties. She announced the results of her work to her scientific colleagues. It was the peak of her research career.

The Curies in the garden of their house at Boulevard Kellerman, Paris. They enjoyed growing flowers and watching birds there. By this time Marie and Pierre were famous scientists, as shown by the cover of the illustrated magazine below, from 1904. A feature in the magazine describes the discovery of radium.

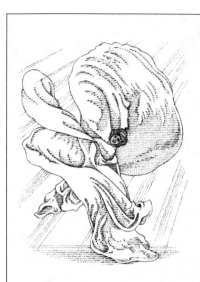

The "Light Fairy"

In 1904 an American dancer in Paris, Loie Fuller, used electric lights (then still unfamiliar) to make her costume glow. She wrote to Marie for some radium to give the same effect. Marie refused, but she was fascinated by the idea. The "light fairy" Loie came to dance for the Curies in their living room – after her team of electricians rigged up her costume! Baby Éve was enchanted, and Marie and Loie became friends.

Rewards and awards

The next year Pierre was persuaded to put his name forward for election to the French Academy of Science. But he was not elected. The French still did not recognize the significance of the Curies' work, though their fame was growing abroad.

Pierre was invited to speak at the Royal Institution in London, where he and Marie were treated as important guests. While in Britain, Marie became friendly with Hertha Ayrton, the Polish wife of an English professor. She also met another world-famous physicist, Ernest Rutherford, the leader of the team that later split the atom. With Pierre, she was awarded the **Davy Medal** by the Royal Society of London. Back in Paris, Marie at last gained her doctor of science award.

There were disappointments. Marie became pregnant a second time, but the baby died shortly after birth. There was no way of knowing at the time that radioactivity might harm a baby – one of its most serious hazards today. Pierre applied to become professor of **mineralogy** at the Sorbonne, but again he was unsuccessful.

A Nobel Prize

The same year, Marie and Pierre Curie and Henri Becquerel were awarded the third-ever Nobel Prize for Physics, for their work on radioactivity. Sadly, though not unexpectedly, neither of the Curies felt well enough to attend the ceremony in Sweden.

Their feelings about the prize were mixed. Marie was proud of her work, and to be the first woman to achieve world fame as a scientist. As a woman, she had always believed in equality with men, although she did not join with the feminists and **suffragettes** who were fighting for women's rights at the time. The Nobel Prize money also helped to fund their research, which they had so far paid for by themselves. But the fame interfered with their beloved work.

The first radium factory was set up at Noget-sur-Marne, in France. Pure radium is a metal, lustrous white in appearance. Hailed as a wonder substance at first, its dangers were gradually recognized as people working with it or using it became ill and died.

New Zealand-born Ernest Rutherford was a foremost scientist in England during the 20th century. He led the teams that put forward the theory of the atom's structure, in 1911, and split the atom in 1919. His work built on the Curies' research.

Success and tragedy

In 1904, the Curies' daughter Éve was born and Pierre at last became professor at the Sorbonne. He had a better laboratory and Marie was his paid chief assistant. The next year he was elected to the Academy of Sciences.

Marie's great discovery, radium, was also becoming famous. One of its properties was that it glowed in the dark. It was also used to cure certain diseases.

As radium's possible uses became clear, its value rocketed. Manufacturers wrote to the Curies, offering them huge amounts of money for radium, or for the purifying methods. But the Curies refused to make money in this way, even though they had to ask for donations to set up their own Radium Institute. Nevertheless, radium manufacturers, clinics and factories sprang up around the world.

On 19 April 1906, tragedy struck. Pierre was thinking deeply as he walked along a Paris street and stepped out in front of a heavy horsedrawn wagon. He was crushed under its wheels and killed.

Chapter Five
Setting New Standards

Marie was devastated by Pierre's death. She wrote love letters to him as his body lay in the house awaiting burial. As a form of escape, within a month she was back at work. She accepted the offer of Pierre's job and became the first woman to lecture at the Sorbonne. In 1908, she became the university's first female professor.

Marie had found a house in Pierre's home town of Sceaux, near Paris, for her daughters and father-in-law. She employed a Polish cousin as governess, and taught her daughters herself for a time. The shy Irène, like her mother, took to mathematics and science. The more confident Éve was gifted in painting, music and the creative arts.

Marie with her daughters Irène (on the right) and Éve. The children did one hour's tuition each day with their mother. Later they attended a private school with the children of other professors. The parents took turns to give lessons.

The certificate for Marie's Nobel Prize for Chemistry.

A second Nobel Prize

Working as hard as ever, Marie noted that Lord Kelvin, a Scottish physicist, had suggested that radium was not an element, since it had been found to give off helium gas, which is itself an element. With her co-worker André Debierne, she continued to make even purer polonium and radium. By 1910 she had produced pure radium, and showed that it was a brilliant-white metal. She even found its melting point, 700°C.

Radioactivity and atomic research was being taken up by more and more scientists. The same year, Marie published her 971-page work, *Traite de Radioactivité* (Treatise on Radioactivity). In 1911 came another great honour – the Nobel Prize for Chemistry, awarded to Marie alone, for making pure radium.

The Curie

Marie Curie proposed a unit of radioactivity, related to the emissions from one gram of radium. Today the same international unit is used – the curie. One curie is the amount of radioactive substance in which 37,000 million atoms change, or decay, every second!

Atoms and radioactivity

An atom is like our solar system, in which planets go round the Sun – but much smaller! The biggest atom is far too small to be seen under even the most powerful microscope.

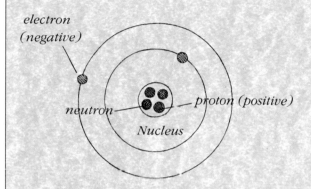

electron (negative)

neutron

proton (positive)

Nucleus

● The central part of the atom (the "Sun") is the nucleus. It has two kinds of particles. These are protons, which are positive, and neutrons, which are neutral – neither positive nor negative.

● The particles going around the nucleus (the "planets") are electrons. They are negative. Normally the numbers of electrons and protons are equal, so the negatives and positives balance.

● Each chemical element, like oxygen or carbon or radium, has a certain number of protons, neutrons and electrons.

Radioactivity is the natural emission, or giving off, of energy from certain atoms. It happens when the numbers of protons and neutrons in the atom do not balance. As the radioactivity is given off, the substance changes, or decays, into a different one. There are three main types of radioactivity.

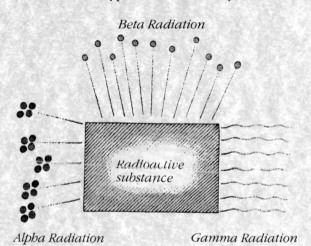

Beta Radiation

Radioactive substance

Alpha Radiation

Gamma Radiation

● Alpha particles. Each is made of two protons and two neutrons.

● Beta particles, which are very similar to electrons. They are 7,000 times smaller than alpha particles and can penetrate substances much better.

● Gamma rays, which are not particles, but waves like light. They are so "small" that they may pass right through a substance without hitting any of its atoms.

21

Suffragettes

The late 19th and early 20th centuries saw the growth of the suffragette movement in Europe. Many women (and men) campaigned for the right of all women to vote – since in some countries, only men could vote. Marie Curie was not actively involved, but her achievements and awards were a great encouragement. This photograph shows one of the most famous suffragettes, Mrs Emmeline Pankhurst, being arrested in London in 1914.

A troubled time

In 1911, Marie failed to be elected to the French Academy of Sciences. Many people said that it was simply because she was a woman – her scientific work was of the highest quality. Her personal life was followed by the newspapers, and there was great interest in her friendship with physicist colleague Paul Langevin, who had left his wife. Extremely upset, Marie fell ill. After treatment she stayed with her friend Hertha Ayrton in England.

When she returned to work in Paris in 1912, she was offered a purpose-built laboratory by the Pasteur Institute. Half of the building was for radiation research and the other half for the medical applications of radioactivity. Radium clinics were opening in many areas. Some made wild claims about what the magic radium could treat and cure. Radium Institutes were also being founded, for research into the medical and other uses of the precious radioactive metal.

By 1914 the Radium Institute at the University of Paris was finished. The same year, World War One began.

Chapter Six
The War and After

Marie Curie threw herself into the war effort. She obtained funds and organized X-ray equipment for hospitals, to help them locate bullets and **shrapnel** in the wounds of injured soldiers. She studied anatomy (the structure of the body) in her spare time, and taught her daughter Irène to help. She set up a course to train people to use the radiography (X-ray) units.

At the end of the war, in 1918, Marie became Director of the Paris Radium Institute. Irène worked with her, studying the alpha particles (see page 21) given off by polonium. The Institute became a world centre for radiation physics and chemistry. Under Marie's guidance, the researchers studied the chemistry of radioactive substances and their medical uses.

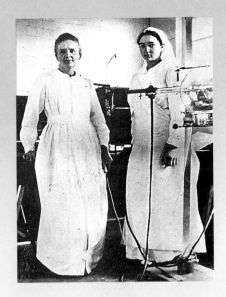

Marie and her daughter Irène ready to help the injured of World War One. They asked the rich people of Paris to give funds for the war effort.

The vans in the picture, called "Little Curies", were World War One vehicles fitted with X-ray equipment. They were used to check injured soldiers near the battlefront for broken bones and embedded bullets. Marie and her helpers obtained and fitted 200 of these mobile X-ray units.

Marie takes the arm of US President Harding, on her tour in 1921. On the far left is Marie Meloney, Marie's journalist friend, who organized and publicised this tour (and many others). However Marie Curie often became tired and ill, and she had to cut her travels short. In the photograph below, she is returning from North America to Europe.

Tours and fund-raising

In 1920, at the age of 52, Marie Curie became friends with another Marie – Marie Meloney, an American journalist. Marie the journalist helped to improve Marie the scientist's public image, and planned to raise money for the Radium Institute by a lecture tour of the USA.

Although Marie Curie's hearing and sight were failing, she carried out part of the tour before illness forced her to return to France. American people and industries gave her money, samples of radioactive substances, and equipment. Many universities awarded her special degrees, and The Women of America gave her one gram of radium, worth a hundred thousand dollars, in recognition of her work and achievements as a woman scientist. The radium was presented by the US President, Warren Harding.

In 1922, she was at last elected to the French Academy of Medicine.

The invisible danger

During the 1920s, the damaging effects of radioactivity on the human body – and on all living things – were becoming more obvious. Many "miracle" preparations containing radium, such as face creams and tonics, did more harm than good. The scientists who had worked with the Curies in the early years were ill and dying. Gradually the hazards of radioactivity – burns, sickness, ulcers, cancers and many other illnesses – were recognized and guarded against.

The later years

Marie continued to oversee the work in her own laboratories in Paris. She also travelled to raise funds for research by younger scientists. She went to Belgium, Brazil, Spain and Czechoslovakia. On a return visit to the USA in 1928 she was given a car by motor manufacturer Henry Ford, and she met President Herbert Hoover at the White House. She sent some of her money to the new Radium Institute in her home town of Warsaw.

Marie had an operation for cataracts, a misting-over at the front of the eyes. She was cared for by her daughter Ève. After further illness, she died on 4 July 1934, at Sancellemoz, Switzerland. A pioneer of radioactivity research, and the first famous woman scientist, she had suffered from radiation sickness for more than half her life.

The case of the Dial-Painters

During 1927-28, there was a famous court case in the USA. Five women, whose jobs were to put the radium-containing luminous paint onto clock dials, were dying. They believed their illnesses were caused by exposure to the radioactive paint. They went to court against their employers, the US Radium Corporation, and asked for money to pay for their medical treatment. The case hit the world's newspaper head-lines. Marie Curie herself wrote to suggest that they eat raw calf's liver. The US Radium Corporation said the paint was not the cause of the illnesses, but it gave money and pensions to the women.

The Curies are often the subject of postage stamps celebrating their discoveries and lives. The star-like picture on the far right is a diagram of an atom.

Chapter Seven
Marie Curie in perspective

A terrifying result of scientific research – the second atomic bomb explodes over the Japanese city of Nagasaki, in 1945. Radioactivity was spread over a huge area. World War Two finished a few days later.

Marie's discovery, radium, is rarely used today, even in scientific research. However her work on its purification, and on the nature of its emissions, helped enormously towards an understanding of radioactivity in general and the nature of the atom.

Atomic bombs

The work of Marie Curie, Ernest Rutherford, Albert Einstein, Otto Hahn and many other scientists led to the understanding of the nature of atoms, and how they can be split or joined to release energy. In nuclear fission, the nuclei (central parts) of atoms fall apart. In nuclear fusion, the nuclei fuse or join together. Under the right conditions, incredible amounts of heat, light and other forms of energy are released.

In 1945 two atomic bombs of devastating power were dropped on Japan, near the end of World War Two. The bombs worked by nuclear fission. Today, countries such as the USA and Russia have enough of the even more powerful hydrogen bombs to destroy the world many times.

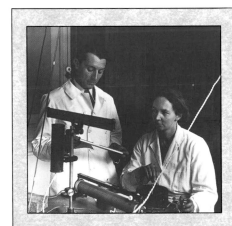

Marie's daughter Irène, and her physicist husband Frédéric Joliot. They got to know one another when Frédéric was employed as Marie's laboratory assistant.

The work of Irène and Frédéric

The Curie family carried on the research. In 1925 Marie's daughter Irène received her doctor of science award, for research into the alpha rays emitted by polonium. Marie did not attend the ceremony, so that Irène could receive all the attention. A year later Irène married French physicist Frédéric Joliot, Marie's laboratory assistant. Their work at the Institut du Radium (Radium Institute) in Paris led to the discovery of artificial radioactivity in 1934. (This happens when a non-radioactive substance is bombarded with emissions, and itself becomes radioactive.) They bombarded aluminium with alpha rays from plutonium, and made a form of phosphorous. In 1935 Frédéric and Irène Joliot-Curie received the Nobel Prize for Chemistry.

The Joliot-Curies' work had also helped towards the discovery of the atomic particles called neutrons by English physicist James Chadwick, in 1932.

Nuclear power

In 1942, building on the work of the Curies and many other scientists, the physicist Enrico Fermi operated the first experimental nuclear reactor at Chicago University, USA. The atomic or nuclear power station followed. Uranium is used as fuel to produce enormous quantities of heat, which is turned into electricity. As a uranium nucleus splits and gives off energy, its parts go on to split other uranium nuclei, in an ever-increasing chain reaction. A piece of uranium releases more than two million times as much heat as the same-sized piece of burning coal.

The process must be carefully controlled in a power station, to release energy at a steady rate. This is difficult to do, and it also produces various kinds of radioactive wastes. The radioactivity will last for thousands of years, and no one really knows what to do with the wastes or how to make them safe.

The terrible explosion at the Chernobyl power station in the USSR, in 1986, showed that radioactivity is still one of the world's greatest threats. Yet through the work of Marie Curie and others, we have more understanding of the atomic processes and the dangers that go with them.

Enrico Fermi received the Nobel Prize for Physics in 1938, for his work on how substances change when they are bombarded by atomic particles.

Albert Einstein, one of the most famous scientists of all time, died in 1955. He worked mainly on theories, using mathematics and writing scientific articles, rather than doing experiments in the laboratory like the Curies. All these scientists, theorists and experimenters, helped greatly towards our modern understanding of atoms, radiation and the forces of nature.

The World in Marie Curie's Time

	1850-1875	1876-1900
Science	1859 Pierre Curie is born 1867 Marie Curie is born, as Maria Sklodowska 1874 George Stoney introduces the term "electron" for an as-yet unknown particle which he suspects exists	1886 Chemist Alfred Nobel (who founded the Nobel Prizes) discovers a type of smokeless explosive 1893 William Ramsay discovers a new chemical element, the rare gas argon
Exploration	1856 Richard Burton and John Speke leave England in search of the source of the Nile 1869 The Suez Canal opens, connecting the Mediterranean with the Red Sea and Indian Ocean	1881 Digging of the Panama Canal begins in Central America 1890 Cleopatra's tomb is discovered in Egypt 1893 Fridtjof Nansen sets sail from Norway for the North Pole
Politics	1853 Crimean War begins in the Black Sea region 1861 Albert, Prince Consort and husband of Queen Victoria of England, dies	1878 The Treaty of Berlin gives independence to Romania, Serbia and Montenegro 1894 War breaks out between Japan and China 1900 Boxer uprising in China
Arts	1852 Alfred Tennyson writes *Ode on the Death of the Duke of Wellington*, in memory of the Duke who died that year 1862 Victor Hugo writes *Les Miserables* 1865 Lewis Carroll publishes *Alice in Wonderland*	1891 Arthur Conan Doyle publishes *Adventures of Sherlock Holmes* 1893 Antonın Dvorák completes his "New World" symphony *From the New World* 1896 H. G. Wells writes the horror story *The Island of Doctor Moreau*

1901-1925	1926-1950

1902 Rutherford and Soddy publish *The Cause and Nature of Radioactivity*	**1930** Karl Landsteiner wins a Nobel Prize for his discovery of human blood groups
1906 Pierre Curie dies	**1934** Marie Curie dies
1921 Frederick Banting and Charles Best work on a treatment for diabetes using insulin	**1935** A scale for measuring earthquakes is devised by Charles Richter

1901 The okapi is discovered in Africa, the last big mammal to become known to science	**1926** Richard Byrd is first to fly over the North Pole in an airplane
1915 The Panama Canal is opened in a great ceremony (though ships have been using it for a year)	**1933** The White Sea Canal, 225 kms long, links the White and Baltic Seas

1911-12 Revolution in China, new republic forms	**1926** General Strike in Britain
1914 World War One begins	**1936** Spanish Civil War begins
1918 World War One ends	**1939** World War Two begins
1922 Benito Mussolini takes power in Italy	**1945** Two atom bombs dropped on Japan end World War Two

1902 The great Italian singer Enrico Caruso makes his first "gramophone recording"	**1928** Walt Disney makes his first Mickey Mouse cartoon
1910 Black dance bands in Memphis, Tennessee, begin to bring music to wider audiences	**1935** George Gershwin completes his opera *Porgy and Bess*
1913 Cecil B. de Mille makes one of his first films, *The Squaw Man*	**1937** Pablo Picasso paints *Guernica*

Glossary

alloy: a substance made by mixing two or more pure metals. Brass is an alloy of copper and zinc.

atoms: the smallest parts of a substance, far too tiny to see under the most powerful microscope. Atoms can be split into smaller particles, such as electrons and neutrons, but these no longer have the physical and chemical features of the original substance (see also *element*).

chalcolite: a mineral, a natural substance found in rocks, that contains the metal copper and gives off radioactivity.

Davy medal: a medal awarded in honour of the English chemist Humphry Davy (1778-1829), for achievements in chemistry and science.

distilled: purified, by heating a liquid to turn it into a gas or vapour, then cooling it so that it changes back to a liquid. The heating and cooling temperatures are arranged so that impurities are left behind.

electrolysing: breaking down a liquid into smaller parts contained in the liquid by passing electricity through it. This process is one way to purify substances.

electromagnet: a magnet made by passing electricity through a coil of wire that surrounds a bar of iron. Unlike an ordinary or permanent magnet, the magnetism of an electromagnet is switched on and off by switching the electricity on and off.

electrometer: a scientific device for measuring how much electricity can pass through air or similar substances.

element: a single, pure substance, such as iron or carbon. All the *atoms* (see above) of an element are the same as each other, and different from the atoms of other elements.

emissions: something given off by a substance or process. The Sun emits heat and light. Radioactive substances emit radiation, as invisible particles and waves.

equations: mathematical or chemical "sums" with an equals sign (=) in them, where the two sides balance or are equal.

evolution: the changes in animals and plants over a very long time, such as the appearance of dinosaurs over 200 million years ago, and their dying out 65 million years ago.

Floating University: a group of people who meet to discuss and learn about topics such as science, politics or economics. They are not proper students at a real university. They meet informally at different places and times, as they wish.

governess: a woman who looks after and teaches children at their home, rather than the children going to school.

laboratory: a place where people carry out scientific research and experiments.

mineralogy: the study of minerals, the natural substances that make up stones, rocks and soils.

Nobel: the name of prizes awarded each year for great achievements in physics, chemistry, physiology or medicine, economics, literature and peace. They are named after Alfred Nobel (1833-1896), the Swedish chemist and manufacturer. The fortune made from his invention, dynamite, provides money for the prizes.

nuclear: to do with the nucleus, which is the central part of an *atom* (see above).

penetrating: going into or even right through a substance. Light can penetrate water and glass, but not wood, X-rays penetrate the flesh of the body, passing right through, but they cannot penetrate bones.

positivists: people who view science and scientific facts as the most important source of our knowledge. Religions, traditions, legends and myths are much less important to them.

properties: in chemistry and physics, the features of a substance, such as its colour, shininess and hardness, and the temperatures at which it melts or turns into a gas.

shrapnel: pieces of metal and other substances produced by an explosion, which fly off and cause damage.

suffragettes: the name given to women who campaigned for votes for women, in the times when some countries allowed only men to vote in elections.

tuberculosis: a serious disease which affects the lungs and other body parts, causing severe coughing, fever, sweating, general ill-health, and sometimes death.

uranium: a heavy, silvery-white metal that gives off radioactivity. It is an example of an *element* (see above).

Index